OCT 22 2002

Y0-BBY-287

DEMCO

Colonial America

School in Colonial America

By Mark Thomas

Welcome Books

Children's Press®
A Division of Scholastic Inc.
New York / Toronto / London / Auckland / Sydney
Mexico City / New Delhi / Hong Kong
Danbury, Connecticut

Photo Credits: Cover, pp. 5, 9, 11, 15, 17, 19 © Colonial Williamsburg Foundation;
p. 7 © Kelly-Mooney Photography/Corbis; p. 13 © Lee Snider/Corbis
Contributing Editor: Jennifer Silate
Book Design: Erica Clendening

Library of Congress Cataloging-in-Publication Data

Thomas, Mark, 1963–
School in Colonial America / by Mark Thomas.
    p. cm. — (Colonial America)
Includes bibliographical references and index.
Summary: A brief description of schools in Colonial America, and what children
learned there.
ISBN 0-516-23931-7 (lib. bdg.) — ISBN 0-516-23494-3 (pbk.)
1. Education—United States—History—Juvenile literature. 2. United States—History—Colonial period,
ca. 1600–1775—Juvenile literature. [1. Schools--History. 2. United States—History—Colonial period,
ca. 1600–1775.] I. Title. II. Colonial America (Children's Press)

LA205 .F5 2002
370'.973—dc21
                                      2001032344

Contents

More boys than girls went to school in **Colonial America**.

Most girls **studied** at home.

Most girls who studied at home were taught by their mothers.

Some girls were taught by **tutors**.

Girls also learned how to sew and cook.

They learned how to take care of a home.

9

Most children went to school only in the winter.

They worked during the rest of the year.

11

Schools in Colonial America had only one room.

Children of all ages went to the same school.

13

Students learned how to read and write at school.

Students used a special book to learn to read and write.

It was a board with a piece of paper on it.

The paper had the **alphabet** on it.

17

Older boys studied math, science, and many other **subjects**.

Learning these subjects helped them to get into **college.**

Schools in Colonial America were different from schools today.

New Words

alphabet (**al**-fuh-beht) the letters of a language put into a fixed order

college (**kahl**-ihj) a school where you can study after high school

Colonial America (kuh-**loh**-nee-uhl uh-**mer**-uh-kuh) the time before the United States became a country (1620–1780)

studied (**stuhd**-eed) having tried to learn something by reading or thinking

subjects (**suhb**-jihkts) topics that are studied, like English or math

tutors (**too**-tuhrz) teachers who give private lessons

To Find Out More

Books
Growing Up in Colonial America
by Tracy Barrett
Millbrook Press

The New Americans: Colonial Times, 1620–1689
by Betsy Maestro
Lothrop, Lee & Shepard Books

Web Site
Colonial Kids
http://library.thinkquest.org/J002611F/school.htm
Learn more about what school was like in Colonial America on this
Web site.

Index

About the Author
Mark Thomas has written more than fifty children's and young adult books. He writes and teaches in Florida.

Reading Consultants
Kris Flynn, Coordinator, Small School District Literacy, The San Diego County Office of Education

Shelly Forys, Certified Reading Recovery Specialist, W.J. Zahnow Elementary School, Waterloo, IL

Sue McAdams, Former President of the North Texas Reading Council of the IRA, and Early Literacy Consultant, Dallas, TX